To: Jane & DC

Run your r
with year!
Hebs 12:1-3

Janet Ragsdale

KNOW

Peace

IN TROUBLED TIMES

KNOW

Peace

IN TROUBLED TIMES

PROMISES AND TESTIMONIES
FROM TODAY'S CHRISTIAN LEADERS

NORTH AMERICAN MISSION BOARD, SBC
NAMB

Know Peace in Troubled Times

Published by
North American Mission Board
4200 North Point Parkway
Alpharetta, Georgia 30022-4176

ISBN 1-59312-111-3

Know Peace in Troubled Times: a compilation of devotional thoughts from today's Christian leaders

ISBN 1-59312-111-3
Printed in the United States
2003—First Edition

Dedicated to

the Prince of Peace

and to all who unashamedly share

His name

at home or abroad.

WE ARE HERE FOR SUCH A TIME AS THIS.

FOREWORD

This book is about the inevitable and the guaranteed: You *will* have troubled times. And God *will* give you peace in the midst of them.

No one is exempt from tough times. God said in Isaiah 43:2: "When you pass through the waters, … when you walk through the fire." The question isn't if you will have difficult times, just when.

Even Jesus, who lived a perfect and sinless life, suffered great physical and spiritual pain while on earth (see Matt. 26:38; 27:28-31).

No matter what type of difficulty you're going through, you may be wondering, Can God stop this from happening?

Absolutely. He can do anything. (See Mk. 10:27; Ps. 147:5; Jer. 32:17)

If He can, why doesn't He?

God is more interested in our ultimate growth and well-being than our temporary comfort. It's not something we want to hear when we're going through difficult times, but we grow and are strengthened during such times.

So, while God is saddened by our suffering, He sometimes allows it.

We all hurt when tragedy touches our lives, but not to the same degree.

Have you ever stood by the coffin of a loved one, feeling loneliness and despair, and looked up to see a special friend? The pain was still there, but knowing a beloved friend had come to walk beside you made the tragedy easier to endure.

In just this way, Christians experience the presence of Christ during difficult times. In Isaiah 43:2, God not only promised that we would go through tough times; He also promised to be with us. ("When you pass through the waters, I will be with you.")

Only God's children experience His presence during difficult times. If you are a child of God, you have the privilege of asking Him to walk with you during times that would be unbearable without Him.

If you're not a child of God, if you don't have a personal relationship with Him, you can change that at any time. God can be with you in your darkest hour. And He can be with you during your brightest days. He can be the beloved Friend your heart may be crying out for right now.

While the process of having Christ in our lives is simple, there are definite and deliberate steps that each child of God must take:

- Recognize that you are a sinner and helpless to save yourself.
- Ask Jesus to save you.
- Receive His gift of salvation and peace.

No child of God has to walk alone, and no tragedy is forever. Isaiah 43:2 has another important word: through. "When you pass through the waters, … when you walk through the fire." Psalm 23:4 has this same word of promise: "Even though I walk through the valley of the shadow of death, I will fear no evil, for you are with me."

You may be passing through one of the most difficult times of your life. Passing through something indicates that there will be an end. You'll get to the end of the deep water and step onto dry ground. You'll finish the journey through fire and the heat will subside. If you keep walking, you'll eventually walk out of the valley.

You will feel better again, though time—and even eternity—may be necessary for complete healing. You may never be the same, but with God's help you can be stronger. Jesus Christ will walk with you through anything you face. And He'll use difficult times to strengthen and shape you, and to make you stronger.

Knowing Jesus may not change your circumstances, but knowing Him will make it possible for you to respond to your circumstances with a peaceful heart.

Have you ever sat on the porch of an old farmhouse—the kind with a wrap-around porch and a swing or glider?

And have you ever sat there during a storm? You can hear the thunder—you may even feel it. You can see the lightning and smell the rain. And if the wind is strong, you may even get a little wet.

Sitting on that porch, with the storm all around you, you're experiencing a great example of peace. The storm's there. You see it. You feel it. But you have protection under the shelter of the porch roof.

That's how it is when we abide in Christ. The storms of life are still there, but Jesus shelters us from the worst of the storms. And He walks with us. Always. No matter how big or how small the storm, we never have to experience it alone.

Our peace doesn't depend on the events around us. It depends on the peace that comes only from the Prince of Peace.

Peace in troubled times is not only possible; it's promised. We invite you to learn from a variety of Christian leaders what it's like to walk through the valley. And what it's like to reach the other side and realize you weren't walking alone.

We invite you to know peace in troubled times.

Robert E. Reccord
President
North American Mission Board

God's Antidote for Dark Valleys

"EVEN THOUGH I WALK THROUGH THE VALLEY OF
THE SHADOW OF DEATH, I WILL FEAR NO EVIL,
FOR YOU ARE WITH ME; YOUR ROD AND YOUR
STAFF, THEY COMFORT ME."—PSALM 23:4

 How do we handle the dark valleys of life? These facts about valleys can help.

- Valleys are inevitable. They are a normal part of life. Don't be surprised by them. Jesus said in John 16:33, "In this world you will have trouble."

- Valleys are unpredictable. They're sudden and unexpected. Jeremiah 4:20 says, "In an instant my tents are destroyed, my shelter in a moment."

> *Problems don't mean you're a bad person. They mean you're a person.*

- Valleys are impartial. No one is insulated from pain and sorrow. No one gets to skate through life problem-free. Problems don't mean you're a bad person. They mean you're a person. In Matthew 5:45, Jesus said, "He … sends rain on the righteous and the unrighteous."

- Valleys are temporary. A valley is something we go through— a situation that has a season (see Ps. 23:4). 1 Peter 1:6 says, "Now for a little while you may have had to suffer grief in all kinds of trials."

Life is tough, but it's only for a while. There is joy ahead if we know the Lord Jesus Christ. There are no dark days in heaven.

> • Valleys are purposeful. God has a reason for taking us through them. 1 Peter 1:7 says, "These [trials] have come so that your faith … may be proved genuine."

Pain can be productive. God wants to build our faith in the valleys. We love the mountaintops, but we build faith in the valleys. When we come face to face with a dark valley, we get on our knees.

PRAYER GUIDANCE: Ask God to walk with you and teach you through the inevitable valleys of life.

TO THINK ABOUT: Recall dark valleys of the past. Were they temporary? Were they purposeful?

RICK WARREN

Rick Warren is the founding pastor of Saddleback Church in Lake Forest, Calif. He is author of the New York Times bestseller *The Purpose Driven Life* and *The Purpose Driven Church*, named one of the 100 Christian books that changed the 20th Century.[1]

Our Obligation

"I AM OBLIGATED BOTH TO GREEKS AND
NON-GREEKS, ...THAT IS WHY I AM SO EAGER TO
PREACH THE GOSPEL."—ROMANS 1:14-15

 John Grinalds was my Marine Corps battalion commander. He kept a Bible on his desk and I'd see him reading it.

One morning in 1978, I injured my back. Grinalds helped me into a sitting position and knelt down beside me. He called out to the Lord to heal me. Suddenly, the pain disappeared. I muttered, "Thank you."

"Don't thank me," said Grinalds. "Thank your Lord and Savior. You have to turn to *Him*."

For so long, I'd had it all wrong. The message God was sending me was, *Put your faith in Me. Not in yourself, not in others.*

I was profoundly humbled by the realization that God was in control. This understanding

> **With God's help, I could withstand any pressure.**

led me to seek a relationship with my Maker. Today, I've met Him and I know Him personally.

By the time I was fired from the National Security Council staff in November 1986, I knew that, with God's help, I could withstand any pressure. While I didn't need a reminder of His care, I got one anyway.

On the first morning of my testimony before the Joint Congressional Committee, a lady broke through the crowd and handed me a little card. My lawyer put the card on my microphone stand, where it remained for the entire hearing. Reporters tried to get a glimpse of the card, but my lawyer wouldn't let them.

Printed on the card was Isaiah 40:31. This promise renewed my strength many times during my very public ordeal.[2]

PRAYER GUIDANCE: Pray for Christian military personnel to have boldness in sharing their faith. Pray that God will give you renewed strength in the difficulties you face.

TO THINK ABOUT: Are you a believer today because someone told you about Christ? Are you obligated to share what someone shared with you?

OLIVER NORTH

Oliver North was a highly decorated lieutenant colonel in the U.S. Marine Corps for more than 20 years. He is now president of the Freedom Alliance, writes a weekly syndicated column, and has a daily radio commentary. He is the author of *Under Fire* and *Mission Compromised*.

Living for Christ in Troubled Times

"FOR WE CANNOT HELP SPEAKING ABOUT WHAT
WE HAVE SEEN AND HEARD."—ACTS 4:20

My life changed forever on an abandoned road in Quang Nam Province in Vietnam. As I led my men on a routine mine sweep, my boot landed squarely on a 60-pound box mine. A deafening blast rammed through my body. Shrapnel pierced my body and bent my helmet flap into a straight-up position. My M-16 rifle ripped in two.

I moved in and out of consciousness, but this I remember: Corporal Lee Gore cradled me in his arms and began to pray out loud. Literally covered in my own blood and choking from smoke and dust, I began to pray, too.

God heard our prayers. He had a plan for my life, and because of my stubbornness, His chastening hand had acted swiftly. But His chastening ultimately brought peace to my heart. March 8, 1971, was the day I stopped running from God.

A Christian influence can have a remarkable effect on those serving in the armed forces.

I'd accepted Christ at 10, but soon began putting myself first. When I joined the Marines, I told God I couldn't live for Him there. Other Marines might make fun of me.

In Nam, I developed a friendship with Lee. He was a Christian and not ashamed. He would sit on his rack and read his Bible. He prayed, and he talked to other Marines—including me—about the Lord.

15

I thank God for placing Lee Gore beside me in Vietnam. Having a bold Christian influence can have a remarkable effect on those serving in the armed forces. I knew I should have lived my Christian life like Lee. And I made a commitment that, from that day forward, I would.

PRAYER GUIDANCE: Lift up the Christian men and women serving in the armed forces. Ask God to give them boldness in living out their faith.

TO THINK ABOUT: Are there situations in which you are hesitant to let people know you're a Christian?

TIM LEE
Evangelist Tim Lee is a double amputee and Purple Heart recipient who served in the Vietnam War. He shares his testimony of courage and hope through Tim Lee Ministries, Garland, Texas (www.timlee.org).

Faith—Looking Back and Looking Ahead

"AND WE KNOW THAT IN ALL THINGS GOD WORKS
FOR THE GOOD OF THOSE WHO LOVE HIM, WHO
HAVE BEEN CALLED ACCORDING TO HIS PURPOSE."
—ROMANS 8:28

My son was in high school two blocks from the World Trade Center on September 11, 2001. He watched from a classroom window as the death unfolded. He and his classmates were evacuating as the second tower collapsed, and they ran to safety as the debris rushed through the streets. I was at Ground Zero minutes after the collapse, searching for my son.

In the months that followed 9-11, I was angry at the senseless death. I was angry that the children in our mission screamed if the elevator stopped unexpectedly. I was angry that my son had the "World Trade Center cough" for three months.

> *I saw God create good from 9-11.*

But now the anger has been replaced with a quiet sense of trust. No one can deny that a horrible tragedy occurred that day. Yet I slowly realized that, for my son, the day of tragedy had become a defining moment in his life. It became the spiritual turning point that matured and strengthened my son's faith.

As I look back on 9-11 and see that God's hand never left us, I am able to face whatever troubled times are ahead. Because I saw God create good from 9-11, I trust that He can take even the most difficult events in the future and bring good from them.

PRAYER GUIDANCE: Meditate on how God has brought you through past events, and ask Him to do the same for whatever you're facing today.

TO DO: Trust in His promise to fulfill His purpose in you through the moments of this day.

TAYLOR FIELD
Taylor Field is a North American Mission Board missionary, serving in Lower Manhattan. He is author of *A Church Called Graffiti* and *Mercy Streets*.

Can You Hear Me Now?

"WAIT FOR THE LORD; BE STRONG AND TAKE
HEART AND WAIT FOR THE LORD."—PSALM 27:14

 I was driving while speaking to my wife on my cell phone when her voice began fading. I repeatedly asked, "Can you hear me now?"

She answered, "Yes, I can hear you," as her voice faded into silence. I hung up and tried again later. She said that while I had been unable to hear her voice, she was hearing me loud and clear.

Prayer is a lot like this. There are times when we can sense God's presence and hear Him responding in our hearts. The lines are clear with no distortion.

Sometimes God's voice seems to fade away.

There are other times when we struggle in prayer. We feel abandoned. We wonder, "Can God hear me now? Is Anybody out there?" The lines seem dead—no voice, no response, no static, nothing.

I believe that these are the times when God is teaching us to pray in faith. He's expanding our prayer capacity as He urges us to keep on praying in the midst of heaven's silence. We must pray in faith, knowing that nothing can separate us from His heart or His ear. Even when we can't hear His voice, He can still hear ours.

Sometimes circumstances overwhelm us and God's voice seems to fade away. Our emotional turmoil cancels our spiritual sensitivity. During these times, God is still listening.

As we cry out "Can You hear me now," He's responding, "Yes, My child, I can hear you. Just keep talking. In a little while, you will hear My voice again. But until then, don't hang up. Don't doubt My love and My concern. Soon I will answer."

PRAYER GUIDANCE: Keep praying for that lost loved one, that deep heartache, that personal struggle that you've prayed for so many times before.

TO DO: Ask a Christian friend or coworker to partner in prayer with you for a prayer that has seemed unanswered.

GARY L. FROST
Rev. Frost is vice president, Strategic Partnership Group, North American Mission Board, Alpharetta, Ga.

A Miracle for America

 America is in trouble and what America needs is a peace conference with the Prince of Peace. I believe America must be born again or we will perish.

America was founded on Christianity. The Pilgrims who came to our shores in 1620 were seeking religious freedom to preach the gospel of Jesus Christ. The second paragraph of The Mayflower Compact states: "Having undertaken for the Glory of God, and Advancement of the Christian Faith, and the Honour of our King and Country."[3]

> *America needs a peace conference with the Prince of Peace.*

America's government is rooted in a belief in Almighty God. Those who drafted the Declaration of Independence believed in God and in a system of absolute truth and morality. Of the 56 men who signed the Declaration of Independence, nearly all were professing Christians.[4]

President George Washington was a devout Christian. Historians tell us that this man got on his knees in the snow to ask God's blessing upon his ragtag army at Valley Forge.[5]

21

President Abraham Lincoln said, "Without the assistance of the Divine Being ..., I cannot succeed and with that assistance, I cannot fail."[6]

Thomas Jefferson wrote: "The God who gave us life, gave us liberty at the same time."[7]

As America adhered to the principles of God's Word, America prospered. We have had poverty, but the poor in America are rich compared with that of most people in the world. God has blessed America from sea to shining sea.

But America is tottering. We are experiencing internal danger. I do not believe that America can hold back the hand of God's righteous intervention much longer. I believe we are ripe for God's judgment. We have had more opportunities, blessings, and preaching than any other nation. But what have we done with our blessings?

We seek peace, but we'll not have it until we have an alliance with the Prince of Peace.

Would you ask God to bless America today?

PRAYER GUIDANCE: Pray for revival for our nation.

TO DO: Read and meditate on Psalm 80.

ADRIAN ROGERS
Dr. Rogers is pastor of Bellevue Baptist Church, Memphis, Tenn. He is the author of *God's Wisdom Is Better Than Gold, The Power of His Presence, Ten Secrets for a Successful Family, Believe in Miracles but Trust in Jesus, The Lord Is My Shepherd, The Wonder of It All,* and *The Incredible Power of Kingdom Authority.*

Preparation for an Uncertain Future

"YOU DO NOT EVEN KNOW WHAT WILL HAPPEN
TOMORROW." —JAMES 4:14

March 4, 2003, was a normal day until, in a split second, everything changed. While my husband waited for our luggage at Davao International Airport in the Philippines, the kids and I made our way outside to meet the kind neighbor who had come to pick us up. After a brief but sweet reunion, I agreed to take the children on to the car.

One moment, the children and I were casually winding our way through the crowd. The next moment, I heard a deafening noise. A tremendous heat swept down my back. Thick *I felt pain and the wetness of blood.*
white smoke rolled over top of us. I felt pain and the wetness of blood.

I dared not look back to take in the scene behind us. Still holding my daughter's hand and carrying our infant son, I ran for the car. My daughter fell to her knees as someone pushed her from behind. When two women fell on top of her, I scooped her up with my free arm and continued to run.

When I reached our car, I knew nothing of the fate of my husband or our precious friend. Tending to my children's injuries and fearing further danger, I did not dare go back.

I later learned that a bomb had exploded and our friend and neighbor had been killed by the blast. We were comforted that he was in the presence of our Heavenly Father. But sadly, many others who died that day are not with him in heaven. They died with no eternal hope, and no Savior.

For those of us at the airport that day, there was no time to run from danger. There were no second chances. There were no deathbed decisions for Christ.

PRAYER GUIDANCE: Pray with urgency for the salvation of lost people throughout the world.

TO THINK ABOUT: Is everyone you know prepared for eternity? You are not guaranteed another opportunity to tell them about the Savior.

 BARBARA STEVENS
Barbara Stevens is an International Mission Board missionary serving in the Philippines.

War Is Hell

"FOR OUR STRUGGLE IS NOT AGAINST FLESH AND BLOOD, BUT AGAINST THE RULERS, AGAINST THE AUTHORITIES, AGAINST THE POWERS OF THIS DARK WORLD AND AGAINST THE SPIRITUAL FORCES OF EVIL IN THE HEAVENLY REALMS."
—EPHESIANS 6:12

The bullet ripping through my left upper chest felt as if I had been hit with the full swing of a red hot steel baseball bat. It tore a chunk of flesh out of my chest the size of a baseball and went through my lung as it cut the pectoral muscle in half. My ears were ringing, blood was gushing out of my mouth, nose, and chest. But worse, I could not breathe—I was smothering!

Quickly, my platoon sergeant and others placed me on top of three dead American soldiers and gave me up to die. Face down in a puddle of my own blood, I could only whisper three words. I was certain these would be the last words I would ever say. They became my prayer as I repeated them aloud twice: "God help me. ... God help me."

Face down in a puddle of my own blood, I could only whisper, "God help me."

That's when it happened! God stepped in and worked a miracle! He not only saved my life, but He completely changed my life, too!

People say it, but war is not hell. But war is horrible. And not all wars are somewhere overseas. There are multiplied millions of "war zones" in our lives—in our workplaces, our marriages, our homes, even in our own hearts.

But no matter how extraordinary the conditions may be or how bad they may seem, the focus should not be, "Wow, what a situation," but rather, "Wow, what a Savior! What a Lord! What a God!" The same God and Savior who heard my dying cry waits to hear and help you right now, whatever your war.

PRAYER GUIDANCE: Finish this prayer in as many ways as appropriate: God help me _____.

TO THINK ABOUT: At this moment, where is your conflict, your wound, your pain?

BOBBY H. WELCH
Dr. Welch is pastor, First Baptist Church, Daytona Beach, Fla., and author of *Evangelism Through the Sunday School: A Journey of FAITH.*

American Fortitude

"BLESSED ARE THE PEOPLE WHOSE GOD IS THE
LORD."—PSALM 144:15

April 19, 1995. I caught the 8:45 flight from Oklahoma City to Dallas, to testify at a congressional hearing. When I landed at Love Field, people were standing paralyzed around TV monitors. I realized it was Oklahoma City they were seeing, and that terrorism had struck the Heartland.

While the bombing gave us a glimpse into the darkness that can grow in the human heart, it also revealed America's strength. In this dark hour, we saw our country at its best.

May 4, 1999. The Oklahoma governor and I drove through an area hit by a killer tornado. In one of the worst-hit neighborhoods, I saw what was left of someone's home—glass, boards, bricks, and a lifetime of possessions strewn about the yard like so many dead leaves. But for me, the scene symbolized all that is good and great about this country and its people. Because there, atop the debris and rubble, waved an American flag.

> *In this dark hour, we saw our country at its best.*

I have never been prouder to be an American; nor have I ever felt more privileged to serve the people of Oklahoma's Fourth District than at that moment.

September 11, 2001. I stood on the steps of the Capitol with other members of the House and Senate. As the sun began to set on the shining dome that still towered over the Washington horizon, Republicans and

Democrats, men and women of every color, joined hands and sang "God Bless America."

Together we sent the message that our country was united, and the evil of terrorism would not defeat us.

PRAYER GUIDANCE: Ask God to continue to bless our nation and to keep His hand on her. Pray that America will be a nation under God.

TO THINK ABOUT: What are some ways people react in difficult times? What is your typical response? Does your response testify to your relationship with Jesus Christ?

J.C. WATTS JR.
J.C. Watts Jr. is a preacher, a former U. S. Congressman, and a father of six. He is the author of *What Color Is a Conservative?* He is chairman of the J. C. Watts Companies.

Standing for Right

A young Abraham Lincoln was introduced to slavery when he saw a woman brought to the auction block. He watched the woman pushed, pinched, and prodded as her potential "owners" examined her as if she were a farm animal.

Lincoln saw what was happening as dehumanizing. He found it so detestable that he had to walk away. At the time, he was powerless to help, but he told his friends, "If I ever have a chance to hit slavery a lick, I'm going to hit it a mighty lick."

God's destiny allowed Lincoln to do just that. The personal consequences were great, but Abraham Lincoln was willing to accept them. Many citizens today owe their freedom to Abraham Lincoln.

> *In an evil and fallen world, there are times when we must take a stand.*

Peace is a wonderful thing, but it's not always possible. God's Word says, "If it is possible, as far as it depends on you, live at peace with everyone" (Rom. 12:18). But in an evil and fallen world, there are times when those who seek justice must take a stand.

No sane person seeks conflict, but sometimes we are not dealing with rational people. Neville Chamberlain believed in the innate goodness of mankind. His desire for peace led him to meet with Adolf Hitler. He returned from the meeting, proclaiming to all the world that they had found peace for our time. Not long after Chamberlain's declaration, World War II was in full swing.

We are to do all we can to make peace. God has ordained government to administer justice, to protect and defend its citizens, and to punish evil (see Rom. 13:1-6).

PRAYER GUIDANCE: Pray for those who are paying a price to protect our country's freedom, as well as the freedom of other nations.

TO DO: Write a letter to someone serving in the military. Thank him or her for protecting our freedom.

BRYANT WRIGHT
Bryant Wright is senior pastor, Johnson Ferry Baptist Church, Marietta, Ga.

God's Sovereignty

"AFTER YOU HAVE SUFFERED A LITTLE WHILE, [GOD]
WILL HIMSELF RESTORE YOU AND MAKE YOU
STRONG, FIRM AND STEADFAST."—1 PETER 5:10

There will be times in our lives when we face great danger or suffering. When these times occur, whether individual crises or national conflict, they are often outside our control.

On September 11, 2001, Christ clearly demonstrated His sovereignty in my life as American Airlines Flight 77 crashed into the Pentagon. Just seconds after impact, I was in corridor 4 on the second floor, just 20 yards from the point of penetration. I was struggling to survive with all the emotions and terror that accompany dying a horrific, fiery death.

At the moment I made the transition from trying to survive on my own strength—calling out to my Savior and concentrating on being in eternity with Christ—all the panic and terror melted away. As I lay there, having truly

The times may be tough, but our Savior is tougher.

surrendered physically and emotionally to Christ's will for my life, I experienced the most peaceful moments I have ever experienced. That peace came from knowing where my salvation was centered and what truly mattered in my life and, most important, my death.

Peace comes only after great calamity and suffering. God wants us to depend on Him, regardless of the degree of drama in our personal and national situations. When we place our trust in Christ, we do so knowing that there may be suffering involved. But through any crises we face in this life, He will perfect, confirm, strengthen, and establish us. The times may be tough, but our Savior is tougher.

PRAYER GUIDANCE: Pray for our country's leaders, that they will be godly men and women. Pray for their physical and emotional strength. Pray for them to have wisdom in their decisions.

TO DO: After you have prayed, write a letter to a national leader, telling him or her about your prayer support.

LT. COL. BRIAN BIRDWELL

Lt. Col. Birdwell is a survivor of the terrorist attack on the Pentagon on September 11, 2001. Birdwell sustained burns over 60 percent of his body, with 40 percent being third degree. He and his wife, Mel, have begun a ministry, Face the Fire, which will help those who have been burned discover God's sovereignty through tragic circumstances.

God Is Revealed in Troubled Times

"CALL UPON ME IN THE DAY OF TROUBLE; I WILL
DELIVER YOU, AND YOU WILL HONOR ME."
—PSALM 50:15

God knows that we will have troubled times. This is part of living in the real world. But God has made adequate provision for such times in our lives. These times can do two major things.

First, troubled times can draw—or even drive—us to God. And there we will experience His faithfulness, mercy, and love.

Second, they can create an opportunity for us to "call on Him" and let Him provide for all our needs. In doing so, He will "deliver" us. And in the process, God will receive great glory. Everyone who sees what He does will come to experience Him, know what He is like, and be drawn to put their trust in Him.

Troubled times can draw—or even drive—us to God.

Each of us will experience trouble. God has chosen to use these times to reveal Himself to us—His people—and to a watching world. However, each of us must turn to Him alone and let Him deliver us.

When we call on Him to help us in our need, we create the opportunity for Him to act decisively on our behalf. His divine help will clearly show to us, to our families, and to the world around us that God is loving, faithful, sovereign, and personally involved in the lives of His people.

Not to call on Him in our "day of trouble" would be to deny God the glory that is rightfully His.

PRAYER GUIDANCE: What is your current "day of trouble"? Call on God to deliver you in whatever way He knows is best. You will be delivered, and God will be honored.

TO DO: Do you have friends or family experiencing troubled times? If they are Christians, remind them of God's sovereignty and His desire to intervene on their behalf. If they do not know the Lord, introduce them to the One who can truly help in troubled times.

HENRY BLACKABY
Through Henry Blackaby Ministries (www.henryblackaby.com), Dr. Blackaby provides consultative leadership on prayer for revival and spiritual awakening. He is the author of the best-selling *Experiencing God* and numerous other publications.

Peace Through God's Plan

"I KNOW THE PLANS I HAVE FOR YOU,' DECLARES THE LORD, 'PLANS TO PROSPER YOU AND NOT TO HARM YOU, PLANS TO GIVE YOU HOPE AND A FUTURE.'"—JEREMIAH 29:11

In a coastal town in Virginia, a drunken father found himself solely responsible for the care of his three young sons. Having just lost his wife to cancer, the demands were more than he was willing to face, and the boys eventually ended up in southern Illinois with people who wanted them even less.

A childless couple heard about the three boys and hurried to the house where they were living. "We understand you have some boys in need of a home," they said. The woman at the door replied, "The two older ones are already taken, but the brat is out back."

> *The doctor took one look and asked, "What do you want with that?"*

There the couple found a young boy wearing a soiled diaper and covered with the pus-filled, oozing sores of impetigo.

The lady pulled the boy up next to her new dress and said, "We'll take him!"

The couple drove the boy directly to the local doctor, who took one look and asked, "What do you want with *that*?"

Without hesitation, the lady said, "We want this little boy to have the chance to become what God created him to be."

I was that little boy.

I thank my parents for seeing potential in me. And I thank God for putting potential in what looked to the world like an unlikely package. God had a plan for my life, from the very beginning. Knowing that gives me assurance that He has a plan for the rest of my life, too.

I am grateful that God is personally and lovingly involved in my everyday life. And I have peace knowing that His love has covered me since before I was born and will continue to cover me through whatever I face.

PRAYER GUIDANCE: Thank God for giving you everything you need to be what He created you to be.

TO THINK ABOUT: Even when we don't sense His presence, God is personally and lovingly involved in our lives.

ROBERT E. RECCORD
Dr. Reccord is president of the North American Mission Board, Alpharetta, Ga. He is the author of *Forged by Fire* and *Beneath the Surface.*

Great Faith or Dinky Faith

"IF YOU HAVE FAITH AS SMALL AS A MUSTARD SEED,
YOU CAN SAY TO THIS MOUNTAIN, 'MOVE FROM
HERE TO THERE' AND IT WILL MOVE. NOTHING
WILL BE IMPOSSIBLE FOR YOU."—MATTHEW 17:20

Remember the story of the centurion who came to Jesus for the sake of his servant (Matt. 8:5-10)? It's one of the clearest descriptions of what faith entails.

The servant was lying at the centurion's house, paralyzed and in great pain. Jesus offered to go to the centurion's house and heal the servant.

"Lord," said the centurion, "I am not worthy for You to come to my house. But just say the word and my servant will be healed."

Christ told the people standing nearby, "I have not found anyone in Israel with such great faith!"

God promises to use life's circumstances to produce maturity.

What had impressed Jesus so much? The centurion never doubted Christ's power and authority to heal his servant. He believed that Jesus had only to issue a command and his servant would be healed.

Later in this same chapter (Matt. 8:23-27), the disciples demonstrated the other faith extreme: "dinky" faith. Jesus and His disciples got into a boat to cross to the other side of the lake. Exhausted, Jesus lay down to take a nap.

Without warning, an intense storm blew in. The waves became so rough that the disciples thought they would die. Panicked, they woke Jesus.

Jesus asked His disciples, "Why are you afraid and why is your faith so little?" Then He stood up and quieted the waves and the wind with a command.

Why was the centurion's faith strong when the disciples faith was "dinky"?

The difference was that the disciples forgot the promises Jesus had made to them.

Many of us make the same mistake in our marriages and families. During difficult times, we forget that God promises to use life's circumstances to produce maturity, righteousness, patience, endurance, and love.

PRAYER GUIDANCE: Pray for great faith for someone you love.

TO THINK ABOUT: What does God promise you—today—through His Word? Will you receive His promises with great faith?

GARY SMALLEY
Dr. Smalley is the founder of the Smalley Relationship Center (www.smalleyonline.com) in Branson, Mo.

Certainty in Uncertain Times

"OUR GOSPEL CAME TO YOU NOT SIMPLY WITH
WORDS, BUT ALSO WITH POWER, WITH THE HOLY
SPIRIT AND WITH DEEP CONVICTION."
—1 THESSALONIANS 1:5

 Uncertainty has defined the times in which we live. As a former Muslim, I understand uncertainty.

I was taught that my evil deeds and good deeds would be placed upon a scale at the end of my life in order to determine my destiny in the afterlife. I never had an assurance of my salvation. The basis of my faith was this fear and uncertainty of wondering if I was good enough.

As Christians, our faith is rooted in the assurance and hope of the gospel of Jesus Christ. Ephesians 2:8-9 tells us that we are not saved by our works, but by grace through faith in Jesus. There is certainty in Christ! Romans 10:13 says that whoever calls on the name of the Lord will be saved.

I was taught that my evil deeds and good deeds would be placed upon a scale.

There are many in this world who are blinded by fear and uncertainty. As Christians, we must remember that we are engaged in a spiritual battle. 2 Corinthians 10:4 says that "the weapons we fight with ... have divine power to demolish strongholds." We need to pray for God to tear down the strongholds in people's lives as we share the hope of Christ in these uncertain times.

As an American of Iranian heritage, I was shunned by many during the Iran Hostage Crisis of 1980. I am so thankful that during that time, a school teacher loved me enough to share the gospel with me by giving me a Bible. Ten years later, after reading that Bible, I came to know the eternal hope of Jesus Christ.

At a time when many Muslims might feel ostracized, we need to reach out to them with the love of Christ. At a time when uncertainty is prevalent, we need to proclaim the certainty of Jesus.

PRAYER GUIDANCE: Pray for those who are blinded to the truth. Ask God to give you a passion for their souls.

TO DO: Visit www.atstracts.org for free e-tracts and downloadable tracts that can help you share the hope you've found in Jesus Christ.

AFSHIN ZIAFAT
Afshin Ziafat is collegiate evangelism associate for the North American Mission Board, Alpharetta, Ga.

True Strength

"BE JOYFUL IN HOPE, PATIENT IN AFFLICTION,
FAITHFUL IN PRAYER."—ROMANS 12:12

Heart disease?

I'm a runner. I watch my weight. Okay, I might eat pizza for breakfast once in a while—but heart disease?

God had moved me to the front row of His classroom. But what was He trying to teach me?

At first, I didn't want others to know of my weakness. I had always been the "ironman." Now, I was the fragile one.

But I couldn't reconcile my secret suffering with the words of the Apostle Paul: "Therefore I will boast all the more gladly about my weaknesses, so that Christ's power may rest on me" (2 Cor. 12:9).

> *When we're vulnerable, it makes room for His awesome power.*

I started sharing with others. And they started praying. And things started happening that I had never seen before.

Recently, as I was driving to work and thanking God for all the things He has allowed me to see these past 12 months, a thought hit me with alarming clarity: Things have never been better in the ministry. But then again, I've never had so many people praying for me. Is this what God wanted to teach me all along? When we're vulnerable, and admit our weaknesses, it makes room for His awesome power.

If I could trade my bad heart for a good one, but had to give up the power of all this prayer, I wouldn't do it.

41

I'm a slow learner. But maybe God has finally drilled His lesson through my thick skull.

Heart disease. My infirmity. The impetus for His power.

PRAYER GUIDANCE: Acknowledge your weaknesses before God. Ask for His power in your life.

TO DO: What have you tried unsuccessfully to do on your own strength? Share your struggle with a Christian friend and ask him or her to pray for you.

RANDY SINGER

Randy Singer is executive vice president, North American Mission Board, Alpharetta, Ga. A former attorney, he is the author of *Directed Verdict* and *Irreparable Harm.*

Why Do the Nations Rage?

"WHY DO THE NATIONS RAGE AND THE PEOPLES
PLOT IN VAIN? THE KINGS OF THE EARTH
TAKE THEIR STAND AND THE RULERS GATHER
TOGETHER AGAINST THE LORD AND AGAINST HIS
ANOINTED ONE."—ACTS 4:25-26

The New Testament church asked the same question we are asking today: "Why do the nations rage?" These believers had experienced an evil conspiracy that had crucified the sinless Son of God. Those they encountered were as determined as any modern-day terrorist or totalitarian government to stamp out the fledgling Christian movement.

Our modern world continually thrusts us into an environment of fear and paranoia. Any illusion of security has been shattered. Our sons and daughters have been sent into battle against an elusive global enemy. We find ourselves in this predicament, not because of our deficiency in international diplomacy or our inability to understand cross-cultural worldviews, but because of our failure to fulfill the Great Commission!

Any illusion of security has been shattered.

That infant church in Jerusalem—facing persecution, threats, and eventual martyrdom—recognized that Jesus Christ had sent them into a hostile world. But rather than succumbing to fear and intimidation, they reflected on their confidence in a sovereign God and renewed their commitment to a saving Lord, assured that God's predetermined purpose would be fulfilled.

Times of war, crisis, and uncertainty are times when people are most open to considering and recognizing their spiritual needs. While the consequences of war can be tragic personally, nationally, and globally, they can be used of God to bring the nations to repentance if we are faithful in our mission task. May we, like the first-century Christians, resolve to proclaim God's Word with boldness and confidence.

PRAYER GUIDANCE: Pray for the nations of the world and for those who have dedicated their lives to taking them the message of hope in Jesus Christ.

TO DO: Visit www.imb.org/CompassionNet to find mission prayer needs for a lost world. Choose a specific request to pray for daily for one week.

JERRY RANKIN
Dr. Rankin is president, International Mission Board, Richmond, Va.

The Purpose in Suffering

God wants you to develop the character of Christ. As God makes you like Christ, He will take you through all of the circumstances of life He took Christ through. Was Jesus exempted from suffering? Was Jesus sometimes lonely? Was He tempted to be discouraged? Was He misunderstood, maligned, and criticized unjustly? What makes you think you're going to be exempted from these things?

God is more interested in your character than your comfort. He's more concerned about your holiness than your happiness.

God not only promises His power; He promises His presence.

You are going to go through dark times, but does God cause these tragedies? No. God is good, and He cannot cause evil or do evil.

Can God use tragedies for good? Absolutely. He can use them to build character in us.

What should you do when you go through difficult times?

- Refuse to be discouraged. David said, "I will fear no evil" (Ps. 23:4). Will implies a choice, an act of decision.
- Remember that God is with you. David said, "For you are with me" (Ps. 23:4).

God not only promises His power; He promises His presence. We will never go through a dark day alone.

> • Rely on God's protection and guidance. David said in Psalm 23:4 that God's rod and staff comforted him. The rod and staff were basic tools a shepherd used to protect and guide the sheep. God will be with you, and He'll protect and guide you.

Believers and nonbelievers go through the same difficult times. The difference for the Christian is not the absence of the shadow but the presence of the Light.

PRAYER GUIDANCE: Thank God for His presence through the growth times of your life.

TO DO: God sometimes reveals His presence through other believers. Is there someone you could encourage today?

RICK WARREN

Rick Warren is the founding pastor of Saddleback Church in Lake Forest, Calif. He is author of the New York Times bestseller *The Purpose Driven Life* and *The Purpose Driven Church*, named one of the 100 Christian books that changed the 20th Century. He is founder of pastors.com, a global Internet community for ministers.[8]

Be Still and Know

"BE STILL, AND KNOW THAT I AM GOD; I WILL BE
EXALTED AMONG THE NATIONS, I WILL BE EXALTED
IN THE EARTH."—PSALM 46:10

 Be still and know that He is God
Be still and know that He is holy
Be still oh restless soul of mine
Bow before the Prince of Peace
Let the noise and clamor cease
Be still

Be still and know that He is God
Be still and know that He is faithful
Consider all that He has done
Stand in awe and be amazed
Know that He will never change
Be still

*Let the noise and
clamor cease.*

Be still and know that He is God
Be still and know that He is God
Be still and know that He is God
Be still
Be speechless

Be still and know that He is God

Be still and know He is our Father

Come rest your head upon His breast

Listen to the rhythm of His unfailing heart of love

Beating for His little ones, calling each of us to come

Be still

Be still.[9]

PRAYER GUIDANCE: Be still before the Lord. Ask Him to show you His will for today.

TO DO: Meditate on God's goodness. Think about His care in times past. Consider His promises for the future.

STEVEN CURTIS CHAPMAN
Steven Curtis Chapman is a contemporary Christian recording artist who has sold more than 9 million recordings. He has been honored by the Gospel Music Association more than any other artist, with 47 Dove Awards and four Grammy Awards.

Peace in the Storm

Our "storm" began one Sunday morning when a young man entered our worship service and began tossing grenades. As we hit the floor, I covered my wife's head and shoulders with my body, bracing for the blast. Three other explosions occurred, including one just to our right from a suicide bomber.

We were medically evacuated from the country. My son required two brain surgeries. My wife had six surgeries on her leg. I had surgeries for blown ear drums. Both my wife and son had three months of physical therapy.

Here's how we had victory in the storm. Immediately, we relied on and experienced God's presence (see Ps. 46:1). With His presence comes great peace! "He himself is our peace" (Eph. 2:14).

An unexploded grenade had landed just two feet from us.

Then we rejoiced that this event didn't take Him by surprise. He had even recently prepared our brother and sister-in-law to handle international traumas. They immediately set up an email network that kept thousands of prayer warriors updated on our condition. Prayers were answered daily.

We held to God's promise "that in all things God works for the good of those who love him, who have been called according to his purpose" (Rom. 8:28). This gave us great hope as we looked at an uncertain future.

When the smoke cleared on that March Sunday morning, we saw that an unexploded grenade had landed just two feet from us. Our minister commented to the media, "I could just see an angel putting his hand over that grenade."

God protected us in the storm. The day our church was bombed, we learned that God is always present. And with that knowledge came peace. We learned that we could have great hope—even joy—in the midst of life's storms.

PRAYER GUIDANCE: Pray for Christians in other parts of the world, sharing their faith at great personal risk. Thank God for their courage; ask Him to protect and strengthen them.

TO THINK ABOUT: How are you doing in today's storm? Are you practicing His presence? With His ever-present help, can you have victory in whatever storms lie ahead?

Name withheld for security reasons

The Promise of Prayer

"THEN WILL YOU CALL, AND THE LORD WILL
ANSWER; YOU WILL CRY FOR HELP, AND HE WILL
SAY: HERE AM I." –ISAIAH 58:9

Though some might christen the twenty-first century the Age of Anxiety, our current troubles are not new. Mankind's future has always been uncertain. Since the days of Noah and his family, Moses and the nation of Israel, the persecuted early church, the Pilgrims, and America's founding fathers, the answer for people facing adversity has always been the same: Almighty God.

Simply put, there is no security apart from Him. When problems threaten to engulf us, we must do what believers have always done: turn to the Lord for encouragement and solace. As Psalm 46:1 states: "God is our refuge and strength, an ever-present help in trouble."

Even during the storms, He stands just to the side.

God does not abandon us. He keeps His promise: "Never will I leave you; never will I forsake you" (Heb. 13:5). Even during the storms, He stands just to the side, ever watchful, waiting to embrace us the moment we again seek His presence. His words to Jeremiah apply to us all: "Call to me and I will answer you" (Jer. 33:3).

Even better, our Father reveals how we are to call upon Him. We can speak directly to heaven through a remarkable gift called prayer. Indeed, the Lord desires a personal, two-way conversation with each one of us.

We are His children. He wants us to seek Him, to love Him, and to spend time daily with Him. When we do, He hears and responds. As we humbly come before God in prayer, He will show us what it means to have certain peace in uncertain times.

PRAYER GUIDANCE: Pray for our nation's leaders, that they will depend on Christ in their decisions, and that this nation will truly be a nation under God.

TO DO: Write a letter to a local, state, or national leader whom you have prayed for. Let him or her know of your prayer support.

SHIRLEY DOBSON
Shirley Dobson is chairperson, National Day of Prayer Task Force. She has coauthored *Let's Make a Memory* and *Let's Hide the Word*. Her most recent book is *Certain Peace in Uncertain Times*.

True Peace for the Asking

"COME TO ME, ALL YOU WHO ARE WEARY AND
BURDENED, AND I WILL GIVE YOU REST."
—MATTHEW 11:28

The Peace Palace, built in 1907 by Andrew Carnegie, stands today as a monument to man's inability to find lasting peace. Only a few years after its completion, World War I erupted. Yet, even at its end, hopeful contemporary scholars called this "the war to end all wars." Again and again, a disappointed world has plunged headlong into world conflict.

A friend of mine once visited the Peace Palace in The Hague and was told by the chief librarian that its shelves contained every book ever written on the subject of peace. My friend asked if the library contained Billy Graham's *Peace with God.* The red-faced librarian admitted that it did not.

Clearly the world's solutions do not bring lasting peace.

He then asked if the library contained a Bible. The librarian could locate only an ancient version from the Middle Ages. My friend donated both books so that the answer to spiritual peace could be found there.

Clearly the world's solutions do not bring lasting peace. But there is a solution. We can have peace, even today. And that peace comes through Christ alone.

Jesus promised: "Peace I leave with you; my peace I give you. I do not give to you as the world gives. Do not let your hearts be troubled and do not be afraid" (Jn. 14:27).

In eternity past, Jesus knew you would yearn for peace. And He promised it. Do you want the peace God offers? He alone knows your innermost needs and can fully meet them.

PRAYER GUIDANCE: Ask Jesus for the peace you are seeking. He loves you and has the power to give you personal peace even in the midst of worldwide turmoil.

TO THINK ABOUT: Do you believe that God's love for you is infinite? Do you believe His power is unlimited? Meditate on God's love and His power. Then rest in His joy as He grants you peace through His eternal power.

DAN SOUTHERN
Dan Southern is president of the American Tract Society, Garland, Texas.

Life in Enemy-Occupied Territory

"SINCE WE ARE SURROUNDED BY SUCH A GREAT
CLOUD OF WITNESSES, ... LET US RUN WITH
PERSEVERANCE THE RACE MARKED OUT FOR US.
LET US FIX OUR EYES ON JESUS."—HEBREWS 12:1-2

The twin towers of the World Trade Center burst into flames as airplanes crash into their sides. Terrified victims race from the Pentagon. A sniper strikes at random in suburban Washington, D.C., throwing citizens into the grip of terror. The news headlines announce that using weapons of mass destruction is an option we must retain.

Pain—human suffering—is part of every life. When it strikes close to home, it often causes people to question the reality of God— His nature, His power, His very existence. Why does a good God allow such things?

Why does a good God allow such things?

The problem of human suffering fascinated two of the last century's most influential thinkers: Sigmund Freud and C.S. Lewis. Both experienced profound suffering. But their eventual conclusions about God were quite different.

Freud decided that God did not exist, that no loving God would permit people to endure such pain if He had the power to prevent it. While Lewis acknowledged the existence of God, he wondered how a loving God could allow him to suffer so terribly, and why evildoers appeared to go unpunished.

Lewis concluded that we are living in "enemy occupied territory."[10] Lewis said that God gives humans free will, but the abuse of free will—rebelling against God and violating the moral law—is what leads to human suffering. Lewis said, "When souls become wicked, they will certainly use this possibility to hurt one another. ... It is men, not God, who have produced racks, whips, prisons, slavery, guns, bayonets, and bombs."[11]

No life is free from pain. The difference is in how we respond.

PRAYER GUIDANCE: Pray for believers across the world who are being persecuted for their faith.

TO THINK ABOUT: Are you grateful for free will? Are there times when your abuse of free will has caused pain for you or someone else?

CHARLES W. COLSON
Charles Colson is chairman of Prison Fellowship Ministries. He is a syndicated columnist and has authored 20 books, including his latest *How Now Shall We Live.*

Courage in Times of Crisis

"BE SELF-CONTROLLED AND ALERT. YOUR ENEMY THE DEVIL PROWLS AROUND LIKE A ROARING LION LOOKING FOR SOMEONE TO DEVOUR. RESIST HIM, STANDING FIRM IN THE FAITH, BECAUSE YOU KNOW THAT YOUR BROTHERS THROUGHOUT THE WORLD ARE UNDERGOING THE SAME KIND OF SUFFERINGS."—1 PETER 5:8-9

The wedding was planned for the spring. The invitations were ordered, the guest list established, the church and pastor secured, and the bridal gown purchased.

But the wonderful event would not happen, at least not when it was planned. The wedding day would find the couple thousands of miles apart. She would be in Georgia; he would be somewhere in the Middle East.

Crisis is not a time to let our guard down.

The day that was supposed to be one of celebration for this young couple would be a time of crisis. When the courageous, patriotic, yet nervous bride-to-be shared this story with me, I was again reminded of the impact military unrest has on all of us.

What can be said in times like this that will bring some sort of encouragement? As in every situation, I believe the answer is found in God's Word. Paul, in 1 Corinthians 16:13, says, "Be on your guard; stand firm in the faith; be men of courage; be strong."

We are to be on our guard, to be cautious. Crisis is not a time to let our guard down. These times are a constant reminder of the importance of vigilance.

We are to be confident. "Stand firm in the faith," Paul says. Our confidence is in the Lord.

Finally, we are to be courageous. Where do we find courage in crisis? In our relationship with Jesus Christ.

In Jesus, we find courage and we find peace. He is our strength and He is our help in times of trouble.

PRAYER GUIDANCE: Pray for the families of our military personnel. Ask God to help those who are Christians to feel His presence in a very real way. Ask Him to provide opportunities for those who are not Christians to hear the gospel.

TO DO: If you would like to join in praying for revival in our land, check out www.namb.net/prayer.

LARRY WYNN
Dr. Wynn is pastor, Hebron Baptist Church, Dacula, Ga.

God's Protection

"HIS FAITHFULNESS WILL BE YOUR SHIELD."
—PSALM 91:4

On December 7, 1941, my buddy and I—after an all-night party—were sitting in the bleachers of the parade grounds at Pearl Harbor, Hawaii. We looked up to see a plane coming from the East, out of the sun, flying directly over the battleships docked in the harbor.

Instantly, more planes filled the air. The entire harbor began to explode, and we realized we were under invasion.

After shooting the lock off the gun shed, I ran to get a tractor to pull the anti-aircraft guns to the makeshift defense area we'd set up on the parade grounds. Just as I got the tractor started, a bomb struck. It blew the bow off the Destroyer Shaw, dry docked nearby. And it *God continued to seek this one insignificant person.* sent me scrambling under the tractor, as I instinctively ducked for cover.

When the dust cleared, I saw that the seat where I'd just been sitting was now gone. In its place was a huge chunk of concrete.

I know God spared my life that day, and many other times in the next few years. But I didn't recognize His protective hand at the time. Though I'd accepted Christ at 14, I faced the entirety of World War II as an immature Christian, living an ungodly life.

I had two fellow Marines who witnessed to me, but because of my stubbornness, I faced the war without the peace I could have had. My biggest regret from my years in the Marine Corps is that I was not obedient to the Lord's leading. I missed the peace that was available to me. But

I'm grateful God was patient and continued to seek this one insignificant person.

PRAYER GUIDANCE: Ask God to strengthen your faith and to give you boldness in sharing Christ.

TO DO: Send a letter of encouragement to someone serving in the armed forces. Include a tract, and ask about it in a follow-up letter.

JACK CARROLL
Bro. Carroll is retired but serving as interim pastor at Island Baptist Church, Anna Maria Island, Fla., while the church's regular pastor is on active duty as a chaplain in the Middle East.

A Death That Resulted in Life

"PHILIP FOUND NATHANAEL AND TOLD HIM, 'WE
HAVE FOUND THE ONE MOSES WROTE ABOUT IN
THE LAW, AND ABOUT WHOM THE PROPHETS ALSO
WROTE—JESUS OF NAZARETH.'"—JOHN 1:45

In 1972, my best friend, Lee, died of a brain hemorrhage. He was 17. We were inseparable and I never doubted that we would be friends forever.

Although Lee and I were unbelievers, looking back, I can see God's hand in the formation of our friendship. As close as we were, we each had our own circle of friends that, as a rule, did not mix socially. Providentially, Lee and I never followed that rule and I knew several of his friends and family.

Our common grief brought us to the feet of our uncommon Savior.

The trauma of losing my friend sent me reeling. I dropped out of school and joined the Marine Corps. One evening after returning home from boot camp, I looked up Ernie, Lee's younger brother, hoping desperately to recapture something of Lee in his sibling.

Ernie mentioned that David, a friend I had not seen since the funeral, had gotten "religious." I was curious to know exactly what had happened and so we stopped at his home. David came out with a Bible under his arm, jumped into the backseat of my car, and presented the gospel so compellingly that both Ernie and I received Jesus as Lord and Savior that night.

Today, I thank God for the good friend I lost more than 30 years ago. And I thank God for bringing good from the tragedy of his death. It was Lee who introduced me to David, and David introduced me to Jesus. And the grief over our common friend was the driving force that brought us to the feet of our uncommon Savior.

PRAYER GUIDANCE: Thank God for bringing good from even the worst of circumstances. Ask Him to help you use every opportunity to share your faith.

TO THINK ABOUT: Do you have a friend who needs to know about Jesus?

RUDY GONZALEZ
After accepting Christ, Dr. Gonzalez returned to school and received a G.E.D. He later earned B.A., M.Div., Th.M., and Ph.D. degrees. He served as a seminary professor before accepting his current position as director of Interfaith Evangelism, North American Mission Board, Alpharetta, Ga.

Peace in the Worst of Storms

"AND THE PEACE OF GOD, WHICH TRANSCENDS
ALL UNDERSTANDING, WILL GUARD YOUR HEARTS
AND YOUR MINDS IN CHRIST JESUS."
—PHILIPPIANS 4:7

Horatio Spafford was a successful Chicago businessman and attorney. He was also a dedicated Christian who faithfully served his church and denomination.

However, in 1871, much of his wealth was destroyed in the Great Chicago Fire. The next two years were difficult. His wife's health began to fail.

When her physician recommended a long rest away from Chicago, Spafford planned a voyage to Europe. As the day of departure neared, some last-minute business developments threatened to cancel the trip.

> *Peace comes only through the transforming power of the Giver of peace.*

Because of his concern for his wife, Spafford insisted that she and their four daughters go ahead as planned; he would follow in a few days. On November 22, 1873, the steamship on which they were sailing hit an English ship and, within 12 minutes, it sank. Mrs. Spafford was rescued, but all four daughters were lost at sea.

Spafford immediately set sail to meet his wife. Though filled with grief over his tremendous loss, when he came near the sight of the tragedy, God gave Horatio Spafford the words of this now-familiar hymn:

"When peace like a river attendeth my way,

When sorrows like sea billows roll

Whatever my lot, thou hast taught me to say;

It is well, it is well with my soul."[12]

How does someone living in the midst of this kind of tragedy find peace in his or her soul? Only through the transforming power of the Giver of peace.

PRAYER GUIDANCE: Ask God to give you the peace that transcends all understanding, whatever your circumstances.

TO THINK ABOUT: Do you know someone who's going through an extremely difficult time? What can you do to point that person to the Giver of peace?

WANDA S. LEE
Mrs. Lee is executive director/treasurer of Woman's Missionary Union, SBC, in Birmingham, Ala. She is a former missionary nurse to St. Vincent, Windward Islands.

Facing Fear

"FOR EVERYONE BORN OF GOD OVERCOMES THE WORLD. THIS IS THE VICTORY THAT HAS OVER-COME THE WORLD, EVEN OUR FAITH."—1 JOHN 5:4

Fear is a normal human reaction, and typically we fear what we don't understand or know. And that usually means we fear the future rather than the present.

The Bible says, "Perfect love drives out fear" (1 Jn. 4:18), and God's Word repeatedly assures us that we need not fear the future.

Some would say I have reason to fear right now. I have a type of cancer that has a bad track record for survival. However, physically healthy people don't survive forever. We're all going to die from something, unless the Lord returns first. And certainly, for Christians, death is not something to fear (see Jn. 14: 1-6).

Fear God and fear Him alone.

Two things we fear are the unknown and our lack of control over the future. Franklin D. Roosevelt once stated that all we have to fear is fear itself. I believe that's true, but it leaves something out: faith. Having faith means that we believe God will provide what He has promised.

There is only One we should fear. The psalmist said, "The fear of the Lord is the beginning of wisdom" (Ps. 111:10). In God's economy, fear of God and faith in God go hand in hand.

Jesus said, "Do not be afraid of those who kill the body but cannot kill the soul. Rather, be afraid of the One who can destroy both soul and body in hell" (Matt. 10:28).

Fear God and fear Him alone. And be confident that, as the words of an old hymn assure us, we can "Have faith in God, He's on His throne, have faith in God, He watches o'er His own. He cannot fail, He must prevail. Have faith in God, have faith in God."[13]

PRAYER GUIDANCE: Ask God to give you the faith to overcome your fears.

TO DO: Do you know someone who is struggling with fear of the future? Can you pray for them, demonstrate your concern for them in a tangible way (card, phone call, etc.), and then share with them how faith in Jesus Christ gives victory over fear?

 LARRY BURKETT
On July 4, 2003, Larry Burkett went to be with the Lord he loved and served. He finished the race with the peace he describes here. Before his death, he was cofounder and chairman of the board of directors for Crown Financial Ministries. He published more than 70 books, including several best-sellers, and will always be remembered as an extraordinary Christian financial consultant and dynamic speaker and writer.

The Plans of God

"DOES HE NOT ... GO AFTER THE LOST SHEEP
UNTIL HE FINDS IT?"—LUKE 15:4

 The following story probably stirs my confidence in God's sovereignty and the power of His Word more than any other.

I was ministering in Vietnam in 1971, and one of my interpreters was Hien Pham, a young Christian. Some time after I left, Vietnam fell and Hien was imprisoned. His jailers tried to indoctrinate him against the Christian faith and restricted him to Communist propaganda in French and Vietnamese.

The propaganda began to take its toll. "Maybe," he thought, "I have been lied to. Maybe God does not exist." So Hien determined that when he awoke the next day, he would not pray or think of his faith anymore.

Maybe God does not exist.

The next morning, Hien was assigned to clean the prison latrines. There he found a scrap of refuse paper with apparent English script. He hurriedly grabbed it and washed it. Later that night, startled and trembling, he read these words on the paper: "We know that in all things God works for the good of those who love him. ... For I am convinced that [nothing] ... will be able to separate us from the love of God that is in Christ Jesus our Lord" (Rom. 8: 28, 38-39). Hien wept knowing there was not a more relevant passage for one on the verge of surrendering to a false doctrine.

Hien later escaped the country, again through the course of God's amazing hand. He has since shared his testimony with many, confident that "nothing can separate us from the love of God."

PRAYER GUIDANCE: Ask God to show you His plan for your life. Ask Him to give you perseverance in praying for the lost.

TO THINK ABOUT: Is there someone for whom you've been praying for a long time? How much do you think God cares about that person's soul?

RAVI ZACHARIAS
Ravi Zacharias is president of Ravi Zacharias International Ministries, Atlanta, Ga. His weekly radio program, *Let My People Think*, is broadcast to 1,000 stations worldwide. He is the author of 10 books.

Give True Peace a Chance

 Today's "peace" slogans haven't changed much since those of the Vietnam era. Neither has the lack of peace.

The world continues to seek peace. Unfortunately, many people look for peace in the wrong places. Peace doesn't come through negotiated treaties or United Nations resolutions. True peace—permanent peace—comes when the kingdom of God is established on earth as it is in heaven.

Isaiah 9:6 tells us that "the government will be on his shoulders," and His name will be called, among other things, "Prince of Peace." Isaiah follows that verse with "of the increase of his government and peace there will be no end."

Peace doesn't come through negotiated treaties or U.N. resolutions.

It is in Christ that we see a Ruler whose kingdom expands, and with this expansion comes peace. Jesus prayed in Matthew 6:10 for God's kingdom to come "on earth as it is in heaven." As Jesus prepared to leave the disciples, He said, "Peace I leave with you; my peace I give you" (Jn. 14:27).

God's kingdom is governed by unconditional, irrevocable, incomprehensible peace. His peace comes through complete surrender to Jesus Christ and His kingdom. When this happens in our lives, we become loyal subjects of a peaceful King who contradicts the arrogance of a fallen world.

And it is then that true peace comes.

PRAYER GUIDANCE: Pray for God's kingdom to come on earth as it is in heaven. Pray that His name will be made known in these days and that as He is lifted up, He will draw all men to Himself.

TO DO: Determine to live as a representative of God's kingdom, showing others the peace that rules in your life.

JIMMY DRAPER
Dr. Draper is president of LifeWay Christian Resources, Nashville, Tenn.

A Call to Action

"SUPPOSE A BROTHER OR SISTER IS WITHOUT CLOTHES AND DAILY FOOD. IF ONE OF YOU SAYS TO HIM, 'GO, I WISH YOU WELL; KEEP WARM AND WELL FED,' BUT DOES NOTHING ABOUT HIS PHYSICAL NEEDS, WHAT GOOD IS IT? IN THE SAME WAY, FAITH BY ITSELF, IF IT IS NOT ACCOMPANIED BY ACTION, IS DEAD."—JAMES 2:15-17

 We often consider prayer a call to get ready to do something. But prayer is doing something!

And through prayer, God often calls us to do even more. As we pray, God will open our eyes to opportunities to meet the needs of those we're praying for.

Our first call to prayer may be for someone's spiritual condition, but God may show us other needs that must be met before the person is willing to hear what we have to say about Jesus. Nothing convicts those around us like the peaceful and positive way you and I respond to their needs. Unless we're willing to meet these needs—whether physical, emotional, social, mental, or spiritual—how can we ask God to send us to witness in His power?

> *In the midst of crises, many people are more open to hearing the gospel.*

In the midst of crises, many people are more open to hearing the gospel than at any time in their lives. And when they see Christ through us, they will be more willing to hear of Christ from us.

In meeting people at their point of perceived need, Jesus was able to move them to the point of their deepest need. Can we do any less?

People around us are physically and emotionally desperate, spiritually and physically hungry. They're looking for the answer. His name is Jesus.

PRAYER GUIDANCE: Pray by name for the hurting people around you. Ask God to give you the opportunity to meet them at their point of need and then to share Jesus with them.

TO DO: Find someone at school, at work, or in your neighborhood who is affected directly by a crisis situation. Pray, care, and share with this person.

JOHN YARBROUGH
Dr. Yarbrough is vice president, Evangelization Group, North American Mission Board, Alpharetta, Ga.

How Should We Respond?

> "NOW FAITH IS BEING SURE OF WHAT WE HOPE
> FOR AND CERTAIN OF WHAT WE DO NOT SEE."
> —HEBREWS 11:1

We are perhaps at greater risk of lethal attack in our homes and communities today than at any time since the Cold War. As Christians, how do we respond? The answer is found in our belief in, and experience of, the nature and character of God.

Our faith is in the goodness and watch care of the God who loves us and whose ways are beyond our ability to fully understand. Belief in God is not based on a believer's understanding of God's purpose, but on trust in who God is and His promises to those who are His children. We have been promised that literally "all things work together for good to them that love God, to them who are the called according to his purpose" (Rom. 8:28, KJV).

We must keep our eyes on Jesus, not circumstances.

I have been drawn recently to the dramatic story in Matthew 14 of Peter walking on the water. As the disciples were on a boat in the midst of a storm-tossed sea, Jesus came walking toward them across the water. Peter asked the Lord, "Tell me to come to you on the water" (v. 28). The Lord did as Peter asked, and Peter began walking on the water. "But when he saw the wind, he was afraid and, beginning to sink, cried out, 'Lord, save me'" (v. 30)!

73

When Peter kept his eyes on Jesus, he walked on the water. When he turned his focus on the threatening circumstances surrounding him, he began to sink. We must keep our eyes on Jesus, not circumstances, and trust Him to safeguard us.

PRAYER GUIDANCE: Pray for the men and women serving in our armed forces. Ask God to bring those who do not know Him to an understanding of His infinite love and mercy. Ask Him to strengthen those who are believers, giving them the assurance and comfort that He is sovereign.

TO THINK ABOUT: Have you trusted God's sovereignty in all circumstances?

 RICHARD LAND

Dr. Land is president of the Ethics & Religious Liberty Commission, SBC. He was also appointed by President George W. Bush to serve on the U.S. Commission on International Religious Freedom (www.faithandfamily.com). Dr. Land hosts *Richard Land Live!*—a syndicated caller-driven radio program (www.richardlandlive.com).

A Pattern for Prayer

"YOUR KINGDOM COME, YOUR WILL BE DONE ON
EARTH AS IT IS IN HEAVEN."—MATTHEW 6:10

The prayer we know as The Lord's Prayer could more accurately
be called The Disciples' Prayer. Jesus gave this prayer to His disciples as a pattern, to demonstrate how we should approach God with our
petitions.

Read Matthew 6:9-10. These first verses contain three petitions, and
all have to do with God and His glory. We are to ask that God be glorified
here on earth, as He is in heaven. God's name,
God's kingdom, and God's will.

We can bring anything before Him.

God is first given His supreme place.
Then, and only then, we turn to ourselves and
our needs. It is only when God is given His
proper place that all other things fall into their proper places.

Now read Matthew 6:11-13. The second part of Jesus' prayer also has
three petitions. These petitions have to do with our needs—past, present,
and future.

- Bread represents the things necessary to maintain life. This
  petition brings the need of the present to the throne of God.
- Forgiveness. This brings the past into the presence of God.
- Temptation. This commits the future into the hands of God.

The Lord's Prayer brings the whole of life before God—our past,
present, and future. But first, it brings the whole of God into our lives—
His power, His sovereignty, and His will.

75

If we model our prayer life after Jesus' example, we can bring anything before Him, knowing that we want, and are prepared for, His will.

PRAYER GUIDANCE: Glorify and praise God. Ask Him to cleanse your past, provide for your present, and direct your future.

TO DO: Spend a few moments meditating on the glory and sovereignty of God.

JOHNNY HUNT
Dr. Hunt is pastor of First Baptist Church, Woodstock, Ga. He is the author of *Building Your Spiritual Resume* and *The Book of James.*

Conquering Fear with Faith

"FOR GOD HATH NOT GIVEN US A SPIRIT OF FEAR; BUT OF POWER, AND OF LOVE, AND OF A SOUND MIND."—2 TIMOTHY 1:7, KJV

In 1933, the terror of economic ruin overshadowed America. Hopelessness grew, uncertainty flourished, and fear became a fortress in "the home of the brave."

On March 4, 1933, President Franklin Delano Roosevelt provided a simple, powerful statement that cast a vision of light in days of despair and darkness. He declared that the only thing we had to fear was fear itself.

Fear strangles faith. Yet, a biblical faith will conquer every fear. When we stand on the firm foundation of God's Word and embrace His promises, our fears are dispelled and the light of His glorious truth remains.

Fear strangles faith.

Is it any wonder David proclaimed in Psalm 27:1, "The Lord is my light and my salvation—whom shall I fear? The Lord is the stronghold of my life—of whom shall I be afraid?"

David was confident of his calling and of God's purpose for his life. Yet he knew that he could not prevail in his own strength. His strength was in the Lord. How true for you and for me as we serve Christ and His church today!

Our days are uncertain days undermined by terror and crowded by fears. Yet one thing is clear: God's call is steadfast and His strength is sufficient for these times.

If we succumb to terror, we will suppress the opportunities God has set before us. He is always at work, opening doors to share the love of Christ. If we live in fear, we may back away from these opportunities. If we are overwhelmed by terror, our witness may be severely diminished.

God speaks to us in Isaiah 41:10: "So do not fear, for I am with you; do not be dismayed, for I am your God. I will strengthen you and help you; I will uphold you with my righteous right hand." No fear!

PRAYER GUIDANCE: Ask God to take away your fears. Thank Him for His promise to do so.

TO THINK ABOUT: Meditate on the times God has sheltered you under His wings (Ps. 91:4).

JACK GRAHAM

Dr. Graham is pastor of Prestonwood Baptist Church in Plano, Texas, and is the current president of the Southern Baptist Convention. He is the author of *You Can Make a Difference, Diamonds in the Dark, Lessons from the Heart,* and *A Hope and a Future.*

Facing Life's Walls

"THIS IS THE VICTORY THAT HAS OVERCOME THE
WORLD, EVEN OUR FAITH."—1 JOHN 5:4

Even as children, most of us knew that Jericho's walls seemed insurmountable, but they were brought down by unquestioning trust and obedience.

All of us have "walls" in our lives—circumstances that immobilize us, that cause us to fear moving forward. But over and over—through Gideon, David, Joshua, and others—God shows that walls that serve as barriers to obedience must come down.

What are the "walls" that keep you from enjoying all that God has for you? Heartache over a spouse or child? Health concerns? Worries about the economy or world conflict? How you face life's walls affects your joy as a Christian and your victory as a child of God.

We can shout the victory—even before the walls start crumbling.

Joshua demonstrated the qualities necessary for tearing down life's walls. First, he had absolute submission to the authority of God and His Word. No matter what anyone around him thought, regardless of how he appeared to the world, Joshua followed God's orders to the letter.

And Joshua had faith in what God would do in his life. Even when the situation seemed hopeless, Joshua trusted the heart of God when he could not see the hand of God.

True faith helps us to see beyond our "walls" and glimpse the victory. Without the assurance that our walls are temporary, that there's something else on the other side, we'd never have the courage to move forward.

But with submission to the authority of God, and faith in the ability of God, we can see beyond our walls. We can shout the victory—even before the walls start crumbling.

PRAYER GUIDANCE: Praise God for His omnipotence and His sovereignty. Ask Him to give you unquestioning faith and obedience.

TO THINK ABOUT: As you consider peace in these troubled political times, is it sometimes easier to focus on the walls—the seemingly insurmountable barriers to the peace we yearn for—than to trust God's ability to remove any and all barriers?

RICHARD HARRIS
Dr. Harris is vice president, Church Planting Group, North American Mission Board, Alpharetta, Ga.

Private Wars

> "DO NOT BE ANXIOUS ABOUT ANYTHING, BUT IN
> EVERYTHING, BY PRAYER AND PETITION, WITH
> THANKSGIVING, PRESENT YOUR REQUESTS TO
> GOD. AND THE PEACE OF GOD, WHICH
> TRANSCENDS ALL UNDERSTANDING, WILL GUARD
> YOUR HEARTS AND YOUR MINDS IN CHRIST JESUS."
> —PHILIPPIANS 4:6-7

Several years ago I returned from an embattled part of the globe, grieving over the hard situations faced by believers there. The following Sunday, I vividly detailed the hardships faced by a small band of believers overseas. As I preached, I could see that some in our congregation were finding it difficult to care about battles being fought thousands of miles away. They had just come from their own war zones—at home, at work, at school.

Whether the war zone is private or public, God is sufficient.

We all have our battles.

Why are we surprised when problems, whether on a personal or a national level, knock at our door? We tell God with puzzled voice and furrowed brow, "You must be kidding! I didn't become a believer with this in mind. This is not my idea of the 'abundant life'!"

But God knows exactly what He is doing in the life of each of His soldiers. God promises us that He is powerfully and lovingly at work for our good and His glory in every situation (see Rom.8:28).

Whether the war zone is private or public, God is sufficient for every circumstance. He has a beneficent purpose for each day's events. So, whether in serenity or struggle, we must cooperate with God, being confident that He knows what He is doing with, through, and for us.[14]

PRAYER GUIDANCE: Ask God to give you peace in the midst of personal and political unrest.

TO THINK ABOUT: When was the last time you thanked God for working events in your life to your good and His glory?

TOM ELLIFF

Dr. Elliff is pastor, First Southern Baptist Church, Del City, Okla. He is the author of *Praying for Others, The Pathway to God's Presence, America on the Edge,* and *A Passion for Prayer.*

God's Curriculum

> "CONSIDER IT PURE JOY, MY BROTHERS, WHENEVER
> YOU FACE TRIALS OF MANY KINDS, BECAUSE YOU
> KNOW THAT THE TESTING OF YOUR FAITH
> DEVELOPS PERSEVERANCE. PERSEVERANCE MUST
> FINISH ITS WORK SO THAT YOU MAY BE MATURE
> AND COMPLETE, NOT LACKING ANYTHING."
> —JAMES 1:2-4

When I was in school, I didn't think of algebra or biology tests as "pure joy." But James had a much clearer perspective of testing than I had.

God wants to prepare us for a career of knowing and serving Him, and His curriculum is faith. He knows exactly what we need, and He tailors the courses to uniquely fit each of us. And He provides labs where we can apply what we learn.

God's curriculum is usually different from what we'd choose for ourselves.

God's curriculum includes:

- enough joy to encourage us.
- enough love to strengthen us.
- enough success to build our confidence.
- enough suffering to force us to depend on Him.
- enough confusion to make us seek His face.

God's highest goal for you and me is not that we enjoy "school." His purpose is to build our faith.

God's curriculum is usually different from what we'd choose for ourselves. But remember God's words in Isaiah 55:8-9: "'For my thoughts are not your thoughts, neither are your ways my ways,' declares the Lord. 'As the heavens are higher than the earth, so are my ways higher than your ways and my thoughts than your thoughts.'"

Difficulties, failures, rejections, and confusions can be God's way of saying, "Hey, I'm over here! I've got something terrific to teach you. Pay attention."

PRAYER GUIDANCE: Ask God what you need to be learning from your current circumstances.

TO DO: Do you have friends or family members who are struggling with God's "curriculum"? Contact them and offer to pray with them.

 DAVID NASSER
David Nasser is a native of Iran now living in Birmingham, Ala. He proclaims the gospel of Jesus Christ to an average of 700,000 people annually, frequently partners with the Billy Graham Evangelistic Association, and heads a full-time ministry, D. Nasser Outreach. He is the author of *A Call to Die.*

Our Purpose in Difficult Times

"FOR WE CANNOT HELP SPEAKING ABOUT WHAT
WE HAVE SEEN AND HEARD."—ACTS 4:20

John Harper, a preacher from Glasgow, Scotland, was invited by Moody Church in Chicago to come to America for three months of evangelistic meetings. He agreed, and on April 11, 1912, he boarded a great ship bound for America. The ship was the Titanic.

At the start of the journey, the Titanic divided passengers into three classes, based on wealth. By the end of the journey, those on board were in two classes: the saved and the unsaved.

After doing all he could to help other passengers, Harper slowly slipped into the frigid water with no life jacket. He clung to a piece of debris and cried out to a man drifting by, "Are you saved?" "No!" the man shouted back.

> *God doesn't promise us there will be no storms in our lives.*

Harper called back, "Believe on the Lord Jesus Christ and thou shall be saved." The man drifted away and Harper slipped closer to death. Once again, the man drifted back. Again Harper called out, "Are you saved?" Again the man answered no. With his dying breath, Harper again spoke the words of Acts 16:31. With that, he slipped into darkness only to be brought into the presence of eternal Light.

The drifting man was saved both temporally and eternally, as he was later rescued that night. Harper didn't let his circumstances drown the hope of salvation. Rather, he used his circumstances to throw out a lifeline to one who had no hope.

God doesn't promise us there will be no storms in our lives, but He promises us a safe landing. We will be rescued from the dark and frigid waters of this stormy life. In the meantime, how are we using our circumstances?

PRAYER GUIDANCE: Ask God to help you see opportunities to serve in every circumstance.

TO THINK ABOUT: Read Esther 4:14. Has God put you in a position—whether a difficult one or one of strength—for the purpose of pointing others to Him?

JANET PARSHALL

Janet Parshall is a nationally syndicated talk show host whose program *Janet Parshall's America* airs Monday-Friday 2:00 p.m.-5:00 p.m. on stations all across America. She co-authored *Tough Faith: Trusting God in Troubled Times, The Light in the City: Why Christians Must Advance and Not Retreat,* and *Traveling The Pilgrim's Path* (Sept. 2003).

Living on the Edge

"THERE IS NO WISDOM, NO INSIGHT, NO PLAN
THAT CAN SUCCEED AGAINST THE LORD."
—PROVERBS 21:30

In a world that grows more unsettled each day, you may sometimes feel like throwing up your hands in despair. But may I remind you that God's people have been here before. And God has always had a plan for His people.

Remember Moses? To a generation of enslaved Jews, it seemed like there was no hope. Then Moses was born and his parents made a courageous decision in an attempt to save his life. They had no idea that God would take the worst of times and bring about a miraculous deliverance.

Remember Elijah? Oppressed by an evil dictator and a pagan environment, he thought he was the last believer left on earth. But God was in control. He had a game plan for revealing His glory to a nation submerged in wickedness.

The world has been on the brink of disaster on more than a few occasions.

Remember Daniel? Israel had been scattered to the four winds, and a teenage boy and his friends were abducted into a ruthless, corrupt culture. But God had a plan, and a faithful few were used to dramatically influence an entire nation and accomplish God's purposes in the midst of chaos.

And what about the state of the world when Christ was born? Moral decay and religious hypocrisy had relegated spirituality to a hollow, rotten husk of pretense and fear. But into that context, God brought eternal life to the entire world in the most improbable of packages: a baby boy.

The Bible reminds us that the world has been on the brink of disaster on more than a few occasions. Although we're naturally inclined to worry, hide, or lose hope, God reminds us that nothing and no one can thwart His purposes (see Prov. 21:30).

And often an uncertain world stirs individuals from their complacency and provides opportunity for spiritual harvest like never before.

PRAYER GUIDANCE: Ask God to show you opportunities for sharing your faith in the midst of an uncertain world.

TO THINK ABOUT: Think about times when your circumstances seemed hopeless. How did God "deliver" you?

CHIP INGRAM
Chip Ingram is president of Walk Thru the Bible and teaching pastor for the nationally syndicated radio broadcast *Living on the Edge*.

Why?

After United Airlines Flight 232 crashed in Sioux City, Iowa, survivors attributed their lives to God. A spokesperson for an atheist organization complained, "Why don't they ask these religionists who claim 'God' helped them, why 'He' lets tragedies happen in the first place? …Why didn't their omnipotent 'God' just fix the hydraulic system of United Flight 232 and save everybody?"[15]

Job asked the same basic question long ago—"why" (see Job 3).

When tragedy strikes, we sometimes call God on the carpet and demand that He explain Himself. But because God is God, He doesn't have to explain His actions to anyone.

> *When tragedy strikes, we sometimes call God on the carpet.*

For 37 chapters in Job, God is silent. But in chapter 38, He asks Job: "Where were you when I laid the earth's foundation?" (v. 4). Then in Job 40:2, God asks: "Will the one who contends with the Almighty correct him?"

No one truly knows the full answer to the "why" question. Anyone who tells you they do is ignorant, arrogant, or both.

But sometimes, we realize that the purpose of difficult times is to turn us to God. C.S. Lewis said, "God whispers to us in our pleasure, speaks to us in our conscience, but shouts to us in our pains; it is His megaphone to rouse a deaf world."[16]

I believe that these current difficult times are God's wake-up call for the church. He's rousing us to urgency in making sure a lost world knows Jesus Christ.

PRAYER GUIDANCE: Ask God what you can learn from the difficulties you're facing today. Thank Him for His **sovereignty.** Ask Him to give you urgency and boldness in reaching our world for Christ.

TO THINK ABOUT: Think of some of the difficult times you've gone through in your past. Do you now understand how God used them for your growth?

JAMES MERRITT
Dr. Merritt is pastor of First Baptist Snellville, Snellville, Ga. He is a featured speaker for the national television ministry *Touching Lives* and is the author of *Friends, Foes and Fools; God's Prescription for a Healthy Christian*; and *How to Be a Winner and Influence Anybody.*

Giving Your Cares to Jesus

"CAST ALL YOUR ANXIETY ON HIM BECAUSE HE
CARES FOR YOU."—1 PETER 5:7

Television newscasts can still cause nightmares of my childhood in Cuba. I recall bombings, machine gun fire, and rifle blasts. One vivid memory is seeing a man who had been tortured by the police dragged into the streets and left to die. Every waking moment was filled with fear, and many nights were spent hiding under my bed.

But in Cuba, I was part of an affluent family. When my family escaped the country in the bottom of a Spanish freighter, we began a new existence as Cuban refugees.

Even the American dream can't bring inner peace.

We went from terrorism and fear to poverty. My new schoolmates nicknamed me "Photograph" because I wore the same clothing every day.

But just as God promises, He brought good from evil, and today I am thankful for the experiences of my childhood.

God showed me that placing trust in material blessings is foolish. They can be gone in a moment. I learned that even the American dream can't bring inner peace. Only Christ can supply peace and hope, and I've passed this truth to my children.

God showed me that nothing can conquer fears except His peace. It was only after accepting His salvation that I was able to deal with the anxieties and fears of my past.

And God taught me that He continually seeks the lost. Before I knew Him, He was guiding my life through a series of circumstances that placed my family among Christians who met our physical and spiritual needs.

Though my parents became Christians soon after coming to the United States, it wasn't until my freshman year in college that I accepted Christ. When friends witnessed to me, I finally understood the love Christians had shown my family.

My first Bible study after accepting Christ focused on 1 Peter 5:7. For so many years, I had been a great worrier. I decided to memorize that verse and make it my life verse.

PRAYER GUIDANCE: Don't ask God to manage your fears. Ask Him to take them away.

TO THINK ABOUT: What burden is God asking you to turn over to Him?

CARLOS FERRER
Carlos Ferrer is chief financial officer, North American Mission Board, Alpharetta, Ga.

ENDNOTES

1. Copyright (c) 2003 Pastors.com, Inc. Used with permission. All rights reserved.

2. Pages 145-149 (adapted) from *Under Fire*, by Oliver North, Copyright © 1991 by Oliver L North. Reprinted by permission of HarperCollins Publishers, Inc.

3. http://usinfo.state.gov/usa/infousa/facts/democrac/2.htm.

4. www.meridanmagazine.com (Quoted from Matthew Spalding's "Independence Forever: The 225th Anniversary of the Fourth of July).

5. "The Diary of Remembrances," Rev. Nathaniel Randolph Snowden.

6. Lincoln's Farewell Address at the Great Western Depot, Springfield, Mo., Feb. 11, 1861.

7. "A Summary View of the Rights of British America," on the panel of the Jefferson Memorial.

8. Copyright (c) 2003 Pastors.com, Inc. Used with permission. All rights reserved.

9. "Be Still and Know" © Sparrow Song/Peach Hill Songs (Admin., EMI Christian Music Publishing) All rights reserved. Used by permission.

10. Armand M. Nicholi, Jr., *The Question of God: C.S. Lewis and Sigmund Freud Debate God, Love, Sex, and the Meaning of Life*, Free Press, 2002.

11. C.S. Lewis, *The Problem of Pain*, Harper, 2001.

12. "It Is Well with My Soul," public domain.

13. B.B. McKinney, "Have Faith in God," © 1934. Renewed 1962 Broadman Press. All rights reserved. Used by permission.

14. An adaptation from *A Passion for Prayer*, by Tom Elliff.

15. "News Report's Mention of God Angers Atheists," Atlanta Constitution, August 12, 1989.

16. Cited by Alister McGraff, *Intellectuals Don't Need God*, p. 104, Zondervan.